CAPTURED ECHOS

POETRY AND MISCELLANEOUS
FANCIFUL WRITINGS

LAURIE S NOVAK

D1198452

For my especially ever patient, loving, gentle husband of 29 years whom I am thankful for each and every day. Thank you for your encouragement.

Also, I respectfully dedicate this book to our ever eternal source of love and light, along with my mentors, *all* whom I have had the privilege of working with over time. Thank you for your support, love and guidance.

I pray we all continue our journey on the whispering winds of universal truth as spirit and soul entwine once more with eternal source to enrich our hearts fully and guide us home. Peace.

With loving affection,
Laurie

CONTENTS

UPROOTED PASSION

I travel to a far off land as I wander through grassy fields. The sun rises slowly above the horizon casting streaks of light and shadow. The morning mist silently floats over the land leaving dew drops on the reeds of grass.

I lay down next to a gentle trickling stream. The sunshine warms me as I close my eyes and dream. I thank the earth for the softly singing birds as they flit among trees busily awakening the rest of life in the forest. I am magically transported to another world, as passion for life is as I've never experienced before.

A golden road stretches before me covered in fine dust. I find myself walking amongst the creatures of this far off land encircled with a feeling of warm inclusion. There is so much I need to know I told them.

In a language I've never heard before they tell me I am awakening to a new wisdom found only in my own heart. See those shadows? Fall in behind them and be enriched with what they have to teach.

We say a healing prayer for you on your journey. Mother Earth will follow and favor you as you walk this path. Now dream deeply and follow the rainbows to where there is no time. Learn the ways of truth, trust and compassion. Be willing to pass on your knowledge to whoever asks for it. Go in peace always and share your secrets to a world which is awakening to a new dawn.

EARTH BUBBLES

Earth bubbles float through the night sky silently passing under the full moon.
Tall trees tower above the forest floor and sway gently in a lingering breeze.
I breathe in deeply and fill my lungs with purified air. The smell of the forest brings in memories of childhood walks in a beautiful nature park. A slowly trickling stream nearby calms my blood. I sense serenity.

Wanting to sleep I keep writing words to comfort my quivering fingers. My chest aches as I try to think of words to express what I don't really know. I catch bits and piece's of dreams I've had and *so* want to know what they meant to teach me. Do I really believe what I express? Why can't I remember?

Listening to the creatures in nature I find myself drifting off into a relaxing sleep. In my dream I am trying to make sense of thoughts that fly through the forest. Was it a rabbit that said to plant more carrots in the light of day? Or was it the red bird wanting me to fill the bird feeder again?

I catch a glimpse of a lost thought and as soon as I capture it, it disappears. What did it say? Why don't I remember my lessons in the morning when I wake? I know they're meant to pass wisdom through to the core of my being. I have to remember to complete my self love activities each and every day. What will today's activity be? I wonder. Will I complete it in time?

The sun is in my eyes as I think of the bright light shinning in my soul. Is that you silver spirit? I feel your tender energy fill my heart with a comforting essence. Soon my heart beats to the sound of the wind as it rustles the leaves in the trees. Wild birds sing to me and I relax. Elves leave me moon drops to quench my thirst.

Cotton woods are dispensing their cotton and it lays on top of a pond. The cotton fairies float down like little paratroopers on a mission falling from the sky. There is no wind to speak of and the sun is warming the air. The humidity is thick and it's difficult to breathe.

The story of long ago is yet to be told. I look forward to connecting with ancestors to learn of my future. As I learn to live in the moment I consider my next self love act to strengthen my esteem deep within. With growing gratitude and thankfulness I maintain a renewed love for myself each day.

My mind of old times is overwhelmed and burned out running ancient programming. Help from affirmations of my mentors, guides, and my scriptures comfort my heart and soul. My spirit flies to the moon and back for confirmation of forwarding my soul to the outer limits of the universe. As energy of universal love calms my inner insecurities I find myself confident in my higher powers' abilities of teaching, guiding and leading me home. I leave my trust in good hands.

As I recite one of my affirmations I look into the mirror of my heart to find new growth. It reminds me of little green ferns coming up on the spring forest floor. The smell of moss and pine needles comfort me as I walk among the tall trees. They speak to me of gentle fairies and elves which live with them.

Coming to a close, my life will tell of many well worn path's that taught me love. A love for myself, a love for my fellow beings, and I can't forget my fellow fairies and elves. Soon I will leave this place and continue my journey of forever, being thankful for the love I learned. In a cosmic cloud of love and light I remind myself that I matter. I won't ever lose hope nor be sad.

THE ENCHANTING MOONLIGHT FROM ABOVE

Lay with me under the bright moonlight.
Hear the calm of the night.
I see the moisture in your eyes.
Hold on to me as you surrender your thoughts to the darkness.
They tell of a time long ago.

Speak to me of your sorrow and pain.
Reveal yourself to me and all you are.
I will hold you as revered and loved unconditionally.
We sleep together soon to meld into one energy.
Dream with me as we fly amongst the stars.

Your source of being is a magnet which centers my inner essence.
I find in you a beautiful fragrance of frankincense.
Your necklace is adorned with crystals.
Crystals heal us as we lay together under the moonlight.
Finding peace we melt together as we become one mind, one spirit,
and loving as one entwined body.

Flesh upon flesh, warm and tender.
We complete our love, light and peaceful being as an offering to the
universe.
Giving freely our entirety to our creator and one another.
We shift our fears far from our minds.
No longer to be down trodden with worry.

In loving, we find the peace and trust we need of each other.
Silently we embrace with our eyes, looking deep into one another.
As we center on the connection of our being, our hearts absorb the
unconditional love we longingly seek.

One on one, in touch with each other.
Falling into an intoxicating embrace we find our reason for being.
With our courage as a guide we continue to seek wisdom from the
moonlight above.
Our faith and trust keeps us balanced with the energy of the
universe as we finally find belonging and completeness.

A BRIGHT WHITE LIGHT

Sovereign angel from up above,
Thank you for your guidance and love.
Your bright white light is all I know,
I know you're protecting me as I grow.

I ponder my existence every day,
Digging deeper in every way.
I accept the spirit soul you've sent to me.
She guides me patiently and helps me see.

Even though I fret and cry,
Struggle, rebel and ever try,
Your love is there eternally,
But I recognize it so infrequently.

Into the abyss of darkness and shadows,
I find my path away from the gallows.
My crimes are erased and always forgiven,
Through the precious blood of the forever risen.

I thank you Lord for your angels who guide me.
Including the one who helps me see.
Send her guidance and strength from above,
To continue in your footsteps with light and love.

COLORING A LIVING PICTURE

It's the lines that see's the story and color carries the fluid of the pallet. It tells stories of long ago, or far off in the future. Sometimes present day thoughts get pushed away 'til a later time. Denial is multiple types of lines inside the mind.

Shades of blues, greens and purples are my feelings of comfort and calm. Reds and oranges tend to raise my blood pressure and I feel a slight flush in my head along with thoughts of anger and confusion.

I love to draw pictures and color them into a life of their own. They utter a language all their own, speaking to me under a guise of love, light, and a feeling of inclusion to feed my beating heart.

Colors, lines and words speak to me in various visions deep inside my mind. As I dream in the night, the dreams make sense, but when I awaken they make no sense at all.

I feel superior intelligence across the threshold of a beautiful galaxy. I comprehend I'm being taught important lessons to help me with the future and beyond. To feel lost feelings from long ago and far away, I need to strengthen my resolve to endure the length of life. Believe that something much better awaits us on the other side of life.

As I sleep and dream I feel clarity of loving energy. Inside the feelings are lost memories. Memories of child like feelings. The need to cry, the need to cuddle, the need of a warm gentle touch. A wish to be carried away to a beautiful garden full of sage and lavender. I lay in the warmth of the summer sun as it blankets me with comforting satisfaction.

Life is ever moving on, constantly changing, always in motion. What is construed as confusion, anxiety, and instability on this side of reality, on another dimension is our heart's anger. A darkness that keeps us restless and edgy.

There is a need for stability and equality among all people. Sincere like minded persons uniting together for the good of all the land and all the peoples. A need for prayer to heal the broken hearts, shattered minds and souls, a deepening need to turn away from old thoughts, and current lifestyles. A time to reflect and heal, a new hopefulness to carry on. The strength of a new faith. An ever loving higher power to lead the way, to trust our higher power with the hearts of children. To be ever devoted to the discipline of our higher power's leading and to be treated with equality and respect. Will we ever see the day?

Turn away now before it's too late.
Look to God to wipe the slate.
Prepare your heart, clear your mind, and stand by the gate.
Mankind has been waiting. How much longer do we wait?

Why did I dream what I dreamt?
There was a lake, a beautiful park, and a river.
The children played nearby as the sun set.
Time to go now, time to go home.

Time to go to bed, time to dream.
Sleep now sweet child, dream of wildflowers.
They grow in the park near the river.
The hummingbirds drink their nectar. Did you see them?
They welcome little children to gaze upon their beauty and smell their intoxicating fragrance.

When the wildflowers wilt and die off they leave memories of their beauty.
One day when we arrive at the great gate, the buzzing hummers will welcome us in. No longer will we have to wait outside. As we take on our new essence we are forever changed from within and without.

So remember these changing times and don't forget, there's a loving higher power to lead us home. There is love, respect, and equality waiting on the other side of this reality. Join in the crusade of an ever loving, disciplined lifestyle and treat one another with the same love, respect, and equality that's waiting for us on the other side.

KINGSLEY KAT

Once I found a kitten not much bigger than a mitten.
He was beautiful, and full of spunk.
I named him Kingsley, and that's no junk!

I enjoyed having him around as he grew to be mature.
But he would run away when I would open the door.
He'd be gone all night long out running the streets,
I knew what he was up to, seeing his girlfriend from up the street.

But guess who was there in the morning looking for food.
Mr. sleepy head knew when to be good.
After a satisfying meal he was ready to nap.
I'd watch him sleep soundly, my beautiful cat.

He stayed with me a good many years.
One night he was not feeling himself.
I checked on him and took him to the vet.
It wasn't good news, I wasn't ready yet.

I had to leave him behind and I heard him yelp.
I held back tears as I said goodbye, trying my best to help.
I cried that night as he went to the light.
I hoped he'd had a good life and I'd done what was right.

COMPLETION IN YOU

As my inward journey expands my mind, I travel through a darkness that holds an unseen light I ever search for. In dreaming, my lips smile as I fondly think of you. I rest in your arms and my eyes light up when you glance down at me.

I remember younger days of adventures with you which complete my memory with happy, carefree bliss. Your sweet memory will be on my mind for eternity, along with the savory thoughts of our past.

My heart aches for fullness and completion. I am open to the energy you share as it envelopes me, and I gasp for breath.

Rolling over, my heart searches the darkness for an illusive light I know is there. As my blood pressure spikes, I begin to sweat, the panic of fight or flight causes my head to spin. As the blood rushes out of my head I feel faint and try to ignore the feeling. I sit on the edge of the bed and realize it was all a dream not wanting it to be over. I feel light and happy the rest of the day thinking of you and wanting you to visit me ever again and again.

THE TRUTH UPON MY HEART

Upon the land, the sun doth shine.
I ponder the light and relax my mind.
As I feel the warmth on my face,
I am grateful for a higher place.

My thoughts wander from my learning lessons,
To a favorite spirit-soul who keeps me expressing.
I follow a path that guides my sight,
Ever onward towards a brighter light.

I want what is lingering just out of reach.
No! The ever loving spirit-soul will teach,
That is no longer you,
What you want is forever true.

Forever true,
A forever truth to guide me,
To sustain me, to love me, to uplift me.
A self-loving truth now lives within me.

To look behind would no longer serve you.
Remember to always look forward to the light,
You'll always find what you're searching for
Waiting in the eternal loving light.

You may not see it,
But you will always feel it.
So when you are tempted or stray from your course,
Look for the light at it's never ending source!

CLOUDS OF MEMORIES

The almighty red bird,
Always wanting to be heard!
Loudly singing a cheery song,
Early in the morning but not for too long.

As the sun rises silently over the horizon,
The grazing animals are the mighty bison.
Feeding on the prairie grasses,
I spy them through my fancy glasses.

The forest in the distance speaks softly to my soul.
I turn towards the trees and walk the timber of old.
Feeling the embrace of mother earth and father time,
I now know I'm safe and protected with love sublime.

I inhale the fragrance of pine, fir, and evergreens tall.
Their branches sway in the wind as their needles fall.
I thank the universe for mother earth and father time.
I am grateful to the deities for each springtime.

As I'm taken to the past I'm told to lie down. Remember the future, I
will be there when the leaves turn brown. Listen to chords of
chanting in this woodland space, your memories move on and
clouds take their place.

CLEARING OUT THE JUNK

I find myself sweating excessively with heat intolerance and withdrawals.
Feeling chaotic and drained, losing my balance, seeing double, fuzzy, and fog brained, I stumble. The cannabis slowly leaves my blood and body.
I'm tired of polluting my body with that crap!

I will wake up with a new outlook on my world once it's gone.
I thank the Lord above for loving family and friends, grateful I have them.
As I suffer through withdrawals, I need to remember these awful feelings,
With intent NOT to use again. Lord, help me!

That sensation of flying blind to escape is *not* a truthful way of life.
Soon I will think clearly about where I stand.
This COVID thing has had me stuck in one place too long.
Sleeping in too much along with missing the friends I know.

I know I'll feel better when the pollution leaves my system.
I'll think much more clearly in order to write my poetry and color my drawings.
Some day I will publish my poems into a little book!
Captured Echos By Laurie S Novak

So, my challenge to myself is to get my book put together.
I'll learn how to go about publishing a book, and share with anyone who's interested. I will send my love and light into the world, with the soul of a gypsy, the heart of a hippie and the spirit of a fairy, my gift!

A LONG WINDING WAY

Guide my steps when I am blind.

Help me see when I get in my own way.

Deep within the emotions of my heart I have sense of self with an absence, an emptiness of a like mind.

I crave a kindred spirit to lead my soul into eternity.

I look inside myself to embrace the source of light.

I have a passion to heal myself with your gracious wisdom.

Please leave me with a kind spirit to fill the void in my soul. I ask for love and protection to keep me safe, that which I need to sustain memories of wisdom and compassion for all who see.

FOR LOVE OF MOTHER EARTH

I see his reflection in the door window. He flits and drinks then flies off into the wide open spaces. His orange and black covering of delicate feather's are brilliant in the morning sunshine. He brings me a sense of wonder as to how he sees the world from his lofty perspective. He'll be back later for his afternoon drink.

The sun is now behind the noon clouds. A somber feeling is in the air. The humidity leaves the air thick with moisture and it's hard to breathe. I sit in my favorite chair out in the yard listening as nature sings all around me. There is a slight breeze in the air as the trees leaves are leafing out into full bloom. It sounds like heaven as I listen to the rustling of the leaves on the wind blown currents.

Drifting slowly into silence I dream of flying above nature's living canopy. I'm a creature of the sky gliding high above to observe all the life on mother earth. As I tip my wings this way and that I dive towards the earth below. I find a tall tree to grasp onto and land with the confidence of a seasoned pilot. I feel a surge of self assurance flow through my spirit and it gives a sense of belonging in the ever greater awareness of the universe. In my slumbering sleep I chant a prayer for the continued blessings on our natural world. I thank the God of our universe for our place in this space and ask continued blessings on precious Mother Earth.

Soon I awaken from my afternoon slumber with a refreshed sense of serenity. With a grateful heart I again say a prayer for continued blessings for our earthly world and the dedication to continue to care for one another.

VIBRANTLY ALIVE

The blood moon is full. I feel it. I have felt it, all week long. A little stress, a little fatigue, and a lot of insomnia. Also, a lot of soul searching, a reflection deep inside into a reservoir of shadows and darkness. Why I am like I am, is hard to find an answer to.

I believe the reason I come back to source is the feeling of joy, fulfillment and, truth, a deep warm love vibrantly alive inside the shadows of our beginnings.

The darkness doesn't matter, it's the development of our earthly body, our consciousnesses, our imprinting of mind to spirit or is it spirit to mind? A process many of us are unaware has taken place so long ago.

As in the likeness of Source we were formed. In the vastness of the heaven's She knows the number of hairs on our head, and has even shaped us before we knew our own soul.

A chorus sang to us in the womb instilling the knowledge of intelligence in our DNA. The entirety of our intellect is enriched with nourishing melodies planted in us as we evolved in our growth.

IN THE DEPTHS OF MY BEING

I walk down a dirt road listening to the wind.
It is slightly breezy and gently warm.
The sky is overcast.
Wandering to a grassy field, I lay my body down.
The coolness of the ground sends a slight shiver through me.

I think of the warmth a loving hug gives and find a loving serenity.
In the deep reaches of my mind I float away into space among the stars.
Darkness envelopes me as the stars shine brightly.

I feel light like a feather.
As I come back to mother earth I swallow her into the depths of my being.
Her essence envelopes me caressing me with everlasting peace and contentment.
I am going to open my heart, mind and soul to whatever she offers me.
She permeates my being with hers as we become one.

MY NOW AND FOREVER MORE

In the now is where I need to be.
But fear keeps me in darkness, as you can see.
Dig deeper than the fear, I'm told.
Go in search of the real gold.

What lies in the past has me stumped.
My old thoughts need to be dumped.
New perspectives are on the rise.
I can't ignore my heart's cries.

In searching the depths of my feminine form,
All I find are great giant storms.
No comfort yet to be found,
Just senseless lie's flying all around.

Where is your pride, someone wants to know?
Do you ever water it and watch it grow?
What thoughts do you plant inside?
Who do you look to as your guide?

Now is the time to start!
Is there gold yet in your cart?
Come inside, don't ever fret.
You ain't seen nothin' yet!

Love who you are.
The holy heart of mother earth lives within you as a guiding star.
Trees respond to her whispering winds.
For in her there is yet no sin.

Forever she has stood there watching, waiting for me to
acknowledge her wisdom.
There is loving truth for me in her kingdom.
Don't ever take my moments for granted.
I have an eternal life and loving truth with you to share, I won't ever
leave you stranded.
In searching her seasoned heart I have an awakening. In an instant
I am secure in her beating heart, our lives are now one, there is no

shaking. Living in the moment is now all we know. My trust in her will always show.

I am grateful to her for all she shares.
This proves to me she will always care. As we move forward I am stronger than before. She has my back forever more.

A LIFE FORCE

Energy is swirling chaotically and disruptively in my body.

I ask loving energy to flow gently around and through my mind, body and spirit to impart healing love for strength of soul.

Positive words float thoughtfully around in my mind with encouragement and nudges me onto the path of my own truth.

My truth, something I've never been told I have. I had no truth. I had no soul. I had no place to feel peaceful. No sense of belonging. Never felt included. Always too young, too small and always unknowing. No brains, no intelligence, no true self. Living in a shell surrounded by confusing emotions, feelings and thoughts.

I was not knowing that what I lacked was a sense of inclusion, love, compassion and truth.

WHY AM I SIN?

Down deep within I spin.
Why am I sin?
Does the cycle ever end?
Will I ever be clean?

My mind is so deceitful.
Who says I'm not clean?
Those damn lessons about sin?
Never ending slight lives within.

Why is the message ingrained with such hate?
Will I ever make it inside that great gate?
What makes us feel spent?
Will we ever repent?

Listen to this!
In repentance and rest is your deliverance,
In quietness and trust is your strength,
No time to flee, turn back to me!

The sin of judgment lives deep within.
The only way out is through forgiveness of sin.
Settle on complete deliverance within my forgiveness, eternal
forgiveness.
For everyone who asks, yet receives.

A WARMLY LIT FLAME

I bask in the glow of a newly lit flame deep within my heart.

The flame casts a reflection, a mirrored impression upon my sight.

I'm confused as the reflection is cold, but loving, caring, but truthful.

Falling opposite my sight the reflection needs nothing from me, it has all it needs from truth.

I find myself lacking truth.

The mirror of truth reflects into my mind nudging me to learn.

Revealing truth of what hides inside intuition, the truth of what will heal me if only I allow it to permeate my heart.

NO FICTION IN ME

There is no fiction in me, oh no, only ego for all to see.
Laughter, fun and games are my folly, please just let me be me, to be jolly.
I am learning with all my might, searching inside, but oh my what a fright!

Old thoughts are falling away,
New thoughts are prevailing each day.
I have a team who is much wiser, that's why I accept them, those surmisers.

Trust and truth are my new found friends.
I know my behavior needs to change, to ask forgiveness and say I'm sorry.
It's not always easy to make amends.

In my heart it was sealed, the truth the elders taught so long ago.
They never lied, they are only true.
They set an example of what is right.

Stay on a path of the loving light,
No longer deny that they are right.
Always be open to their instruction.

As healing comes into my soul, my eyes open to see the light.
From this day forward, I will travel,
To tread lightly, and not become unraveled.

I will say my peace and move along.
I'll keep it simple, I'll keep it strong.
Ever grateful to those of old, who gave me love, who gave me song.

MINDFUL IMAGININGS

The chaotic pecking order of authority brings no harmony in a time of great need across the land.

As an innate need rises from within the masses of our collective conscientiousness we look to a higher power for healing, peace and direction.

As I sit in meditation to slow my heart rate, my mind wanders to and fro across the expanse of imaginings, ever ready to calm itself, but in my reality it never really does. My imaginings bring about reality of thought, reality of life.

Wherever we are in our journey, our growth is dependent on becoming one with our higher power, our higher selves.

What is put out to the universe comes full circle in a life span of generations.

I am reminded, although not always grounded in my lessons from my days past, when looking to a higher power, God is a secure presence in knowing I am loved and included in a collective network of unconditional love for all to partake of. We all have the same innate needs as humans.

In saying I have no peace within is not totally accurate, because as I grow and learn my way, peace becomes a byproduct of that journey.

As a human creature living with an ever curious nature as to what my spirituality is teaching me, I look forward to completing my wanderings with peaceful contemplation's.

TEXTURES OF MY MIND

There is a hummingbird in the other room, along with an angel, an eagle, and a butterfly. I see them on the plaster textured walls. They're all in flight. Endless in their flight across time, they are beautiful in there own dimension. Rainbow colors surround their essence as they float across the walls and into my mind.

I join them as I glide in the vastness of the universe. In depths of darkness we hold space for one another and connect our energies as the light from our union brightens the dark expanse. I feel endless loving energies passing through us. As we dance in flight our hearts are one, our thoughts are one and we are eternal in being.

A SINGLE BREATH

Today I just breathe, practicing the four, seven, eight technique.

Inhale, in through the nose, out through the mouth.

As I lie here listening to softly playing music I imagine I'm flying high above the ocean watching the waves rise and fall as they lap the shoreline.

As I breathe deeply I become lightheaded, closing my eyes as I relax, floating among the bright white clouds.

The higher I fly, the thinner the air, as I almost lose consciousness. Just on the brink of blacking out I roll into a dive to speed ever faster toward earth. I come out into a full on glide dipping the tips of my wings on the ocean's surface.

Feeling freer than ever, I find a new confidence I've not felt before. Looking up, I thank Father Universe for allowing me to fly freely in his presence.

Even when I am alone, with the sky to myself, I reflect upon the memory of His love as it fills my soul.

With the next several breaths, I intently listen to my heartbeat as I feel the rise and fall of my chest. As my diaphragm opens fully I can inhale to depths I've only dreamed of. I relax to sleep as I am transported to another dimension where time stands still.

WHEN YOU ARE YOUNG YOU WILL KNOW

See the walls you've so carefully built up? You don't need them, you are safe.
See that ladder over there? You will find it sturdy enough to climb up and over those walls. But you mustn't cheat and walk around. No, the walls are to be scaled with the confidence of a knight in shinning armor.

As you climb down the other side you find a fragrant earthly garden in which you at once feel calm. It's most beautiful and calming. There is no anxiety here, there is no pain here, only spirits of laughing crickets and winging dragonfly's.

In the garden is an out of place sundial which points in the direction of a castle in the distance. You have come far, a quiet voice whispers in your mind. The keys are waiting for you in the door, when you turn the key enter in.

Inside a towering turret you will find a lingering thought only you will discover and understand. That thought contains all the knowledge you seek of your inner universe. We bring the walls of our insecurities down as we grow into our inner truth. While discerning your new found wisdom, you will regress inward to grow wiser and in turn, your shadow will grow younger and longer.

Remember the anxiety and pain is temporary. Future patterns old and decrepit cannot stop your creative nature. Once again you feel complete as old ways are surrendered. You dig deeper inward as the universe sends love along with eternal knowledge from far and wide. You create and absorb all that is possible.

As you grow, your old future thoughts drift aloft to be replaced by sage beliefs and enlightenment. Within the confines of our hearts and minds we are forever learning our true thoughts and imaginings. The eternal knowing protects and guides us as we bring the walls of our insecurities tumbling down replaced by the curious lingering thought we discovered in that towering turret. In *loving* what lives inside you, you will find your true self. In *believing* what lives inside us, always thank the sacred energy for sharing the essence of a lingering thought.

Moonbeams and stardust dance aloft once again as you find yourself looking to the moon as it rises. You give thanks to the moon as the stars rise to greet you and welcome you to dream within the jovial universe. As we grow in our journey, be ever grateful to our sacred energy for sharing dreams of compassion, truth, love and light. While we continue our travels be ever thankful for the life we are given and always be willing to share with others that same loving energy. The truth lives within us now and always, discovered as a lingering thought embedded in the confines of our inner consciousness.

HIGHER VIBRATIONS

The persons I find myself attracted to vibrate at such a higher (or different) vibration than I do. We will never be compatible.

I will *see* how they differ from me and how I differ from them, but they will never find my vibration compatible with theirs, nor will they find mine attractive or satisfying.

What do I take away from that? I find it depressing because they *do* vibrate higher, it's just their nature, a part of life's pecking order. It's just a matter of the circle of life, human life, the organic living vessel in which we reside.

Our spirit and soul is locked up in our human body to experience all the things human and to what end? Why do we need all these experiences if we are really just a spiritual energy to float amongst the stars and ruins of the galaxy?

TO WHAT END?
The lessons of life we learn are valuable and I look forward to being enlightened by these lessons.

As these lessons protect us we assimilate their wisdom which is securely kept in our hearts for all eternity.

I, do, however have an innate need for my higher power to take me in and comfort my weary spirit and lead me into a kind unity of self-love, self-compassion, and self-accountability, a belief in 'self'.

I do respect the higher vibes of all living creatures. Deep inside my subconscious I 'know' there is an intelligence to each encounter we have and I respect that intuition and take it to heart, where I keep it to comfort me in times of low vibrational tides.

Does that mean I'm just a lowly vibrational being with no direction? No, that is my previous programming talking. I believe my vibration is now stronger than that.

The more encounters we have with what comes our way in life we inherit that growth along the way.

MY RESPONSIBILITY

It's not my job to hold someone else accountable. It is the responsibility for that person to hold themselves accountable for their own vibrational attitude.

As I evolve, my higher self will continue to teach me invaluable lessons. As the energy of the universe evolves, we find ourselves in an exciting time filled with compatible camaraderie in a world of loving, caring, nurturing souls on the same journey.

May we all awaken to find our gifts, talents, intuition, and ever-loving essence, to integrate with one another in unison to fulfill our destinies.

HE KEEPS THE HOME FIRES BURNING

He's such an easy goin' type of guy,
He loves me without end.
His path is ever humble,
He's gentle as the wind.

Remembering every now and then,
I think of special times,
The love he shows me without fail,
Until the very end.

As times slips by all too soon,
I sense his love with each passing moon.
Up above in the sky so ever blue,
I'm always thankful for me and you!

A TRIP TO THE STORE

Thinking about what I want on my plate, I plan a trip into town, soon I'm out the gate.
Bread, buns, sweet & sour sauce, and hash browns sound great.
With my mouth watering I suddenly think,
Toilet paper is on the list, too, I hope I don't stink.

Down to our last roll, this becomes my desire,
I hope they have some, cuz I have some food ready to expire!
When I get to town, I don my mask,
Ever ready to accomplish my task!

As I follow the arrows and walk the aisles, I some how don't feel this is free style.
But just to be safe, I hurry along, and choose the toilet paper that doesn't chafe.
I'm almost there, the finish line is in sight.
Pay the bill, bag the goods, I'm ready for some afternoon delight!

Soon I'm home and feel relief, sitting on that porcelain throne.
With a gentle wipe, the waste is gone, but not without a painful groan.
I held it as long as I could walking around that store.
But what a good feeling it brings knowing they got more!

GRATEFUL EMERGING THOUGHT PATTERNS

What Does The Moon Say To You?

Do you love all your children as I love you, she asks? Do you clothe them in bright white light as I do? The light of enlightenment is passed on.
In the evening time while the flowers sleep, fairies sprinkle golden fairy dust upon their blossoms. When the bees light upon them in the morning sun, the fairy dust sticks to the bees. They fly back to the hive and share the good nourishment with the entire hive. As they all know, it's the moon who sends the fairies to help dust the crops.

On the edge of an ancient lake a wise old crab scurries across the beach inland to escape the hot noon day sun. The sands glitter in the sunlight as tiny glassy pinpoints of light, which is actually rare golden fairy dust. As he hollows out a hole in the sand, he digs in for an afternoon siesta, under an even older willow tree. As the old crab sleeps he assimilates the knowledge of the elderly willow and beyond.

In the willow tree an owl is resting. He sits tall and high above the forest floor. He turns his head slowly left to right, waiting. He had heard this was where it was going to take place. Under the full moon, for all creation to par take the loving knowledge of a spiritual essence soon to be passed on to our collective conscientiousness.

To find this place, the owl flew many moons, many centuries, many new moons, and many generations. As he flew he gathered valuable knowledge, ancient thoughts, felt fabulous fleeting emotions, envisioned colorful energetic waves.

The waves dance across eternity giving birth to additional millions. Beautiful energetic waves find their way to our dimension through loving thought patterns. As in the ever and always, there is yet another hopeful soul eager to learn and love. All is, as is once again in life, we are grateful and thank you, Mother moon for your guidance. All of life is found again in eternal harmony.

LEARNING OF YOURSELF

I've lost myself again in my confused chaos.
I want to write a poem, one that tells a story.
Nothing new or anything perhaps already said,
Just passing sentiments thought long dead.

In lingering thoughts that lie deeply dormant,
A panicked little girl-child needs released.
She sits listening in perfect silence.
She waits upon the lunar cycle as her guiding pilot.

The knowledge you seek will come forth as a raging river under a full moon. Strength of courage will come in the form of spiritual insight. Be comforted by the light from above, it will follow you during your journey. Trust your vessel to take you on through the moonlight. Your spirit will burn like fire absorbed from the pages of wisdom deep within the shadows of midnight. The fire will never burn out, is all she said.

I'm ever conscience of being empty inside, alone in my own wavering energy. As water quenches my thirst, my heart is only quenched with eternal wisdom. The discerning heart seeks true knowledge. Always read and believe the living words that shine ever bright, they signal you to awaken. Your emptiness yearns to know the living wisdom that lives eternally.

I move forward in a tenacious loving manner ever consistent within my being. I ask for guiding counsel with a love to accept it unfailingly, and a willing heart with a steady spirit to continue living within the loving energy of the universe.

WAVERING WATERS, WIND AND WONDERS

The pond was showing slight ripples from a mild westerly wind. Small fish nipped at the surface in search of easy pickin's, as small insects temped their hunger swarming above the water's surface.

Watching nature alive and active, I ponder the dive under the pond's surface. I've been down to the bottom of this little watering hole and touched the bottom which buried my hand in muck about a foot deep. It startled me to wonder what lie's below that dark mire. I searched for the solid bottom, but didn't find it. Just muck. I swam quickly back up to the surface, my heart racing.

I toweled off and sat in the recliner sunbathing and warming up. I was just about asleep when I heard a loud splash come from the pond. I looked over as the splash burst up like a fountain, several feet in the air. It was a spectacle to see, actually, because the water was a bright greenish blue, glowing with a bright light in the center. It disappeared as quick as it appeared.

At this point I pinched myself to be sure I wasn't asleep. What did I just witness?
I'd thought nothing of it, had I just woke up from a wild dream. And to think I was just swimming there half an hour ago. I didn't sense anything different during my swim. I have definitely never seen anything like it before. Ever!

I decide to put it to the back of my mind, because I want to enjoy my lovely little pond! I love to swim in the chilly cold blackish blue water. I usually just float on an inner tube to get sun baked in the summer time sun. Sometimes I'll actually swim around in my swim goggles and scuba flippers, spying what's below me in the murky green water.

Other days I'll lay on the floaty belly-side down to watch the blue-gills come to me and nibble me. As I swat at them they swim down through the seaweed and try to hide. I float all the way around the perimeter of the pond studying all the marine life of the pond. I see lot's of weeds, little minnows, blue-gill, snails; and the way the sun penetrates the water is always spectacular! I could just get lost in that pond!

About a week later I decided to try a little swim in the pond. I grab my swim goggles and fins and head off the end of the dock. I was excited to be back with my old friend and in my hast I hit the bottom feet first! I didn't jump out far enough! As I hit bottom the jolt punched a hole into another world. I feel a strong circling vortex pulling me and spinning me as I blackout. When I come to, instead of heading down towards the bottom, I come up from the bottom and gasped for air! When I get my bearings, I realize I'm no longer in my beloved little pond.

KINDRED LOVER

A kindred heart is waiting inside, once again ready to play.

Once I was empty but now I am old.

When did I awaken from my slumbering self?

When truth comes up with loving knowledge, sands of time pass through my soul.

The most wonderful dance of all the universe is flowing across the sky.

A kindred lover who knows mysterious ways pulls me in.

I like what is happening here inside my mind and body.

This kindred lover tells me memories I've long forgotten.

The knowledge of who I am, why I am.

I acknowledge my lover and know that I hunger.

Let's have a virtual rendezvous just you and me.

We'll tell each other our dreams.

Maybe one day hold each other.

I don't know why I feel this way.

There's so much to say.

So let's look each other in the eyes and make a pact to fall in love.

Once in my mind you have my full attention.

To know you is to want you.

Let's entwine our hearts together in love virtually now and forever.

Accompany me across your reality with thoughts of yesterday.

Pass your passions through my heart. I would love that!

LOOK INSIDE THE LIGHT

My words are alive intended to speak to you.

They live with their own authenticity.

Words on a page that stir in you a great debate.

Reach inside yourself to see what lies within.

Do you have the ability to feel?

What is it you seek in the cobwebs of your soul?

Are you comfortable with who you find?

Will this person provide, protect and nurture you?

Does your spirit crave a change?

Come take my hand and leave behind the old behaviors.

Seek out that which makes you calm.

Breathe in a connection that's there without seeing.

Become one with the challenge and focus on the song in your soul.

Know that you're loved and cared for by someone who lingers deep within your heart.

Find the light that flickers within and without.

Sing a song of hope and honor for your angels.

Remind yourself that you are life worth living.

PASSION IN YOUR WORDS

I see you.
I see one connection.
One ancestral community.

You work hard.
You work long.
Your success is therefore a triumph.

All who hear your music feel your message.
You're authentically loving and aware.
I admire and respect your sovereign spirit.

Thank you for sharing your innermost thoughts and feelings.
I do understand and feel your love.
Continue on your path and you will reap the serenity you deserve.

THE GREAT GIFT THAT YOU ARE

You inspire and challenge me.

The spark within you reaches out to me.

I find myself deeply engaged with a greater understanding but still in need.

Continually communicating on a specific level I have a certain awareness, although there's always another dimension to achieve.

You challenge that awareness to punch a hole in my subconsciousness to find the answers I seek.

Dig deeper into your island of solitude.

Find the child who lives within.

Reach past the shadows and darkness that fear has built.

Knock down the lies and misinformation.

Thank the sovereign powers that be who show you the way.

Find the light above the waves and soar through the clouds.

What you seek is beyond what lies in your heart.

Choose now the great gift that awaits you on the other side of the winds of time.

LSN 5·17·2020

ABANDONED WHISPERS

Abandoned whispers echoing through time touch my mind with truth.

On the horizon a comet soars past the sun and the moon as a mysterious consciousness evolves.

A sense of urgency is on the rise.

What will is being done? Whose understanding do you know?

As eternal as the winds of truth darkness fills the soul of hell.

Sacred and solitary love at the core, I soar inward towards a single point of light.

A searing truth from spirit soul says it's time to depart.

Willfully and knowingly we withdraw.

But not without making a pact up above with the sky so blue.

Our lessons are learned now and forever more, feeling blessed we say adieu.

ABOUT THE AUTHOR

Laurie S Novak

Born and raised in Wyandotte, Michigan, Laurie is the youngest daughter of four. Her education was through high school and one year of community college with an interest in forestry. She loves walks in nature and photography.

Interested in playing guitar in her teenage years, she took lessons from her father who was a musician and taught music at the Wyandotte Conservatory of Music. She also took beginning guitar in her senior year of high school.

After retirement she took an interest in her local senior community center where she volunteers. She also enjoys participating in Bingo, Euchre, Pinochle, Yoga, Mahjong, and of course playing her guitar on certain days with a sing along entitled Lyric's with Laurie.

During the lock down of the Covid 19 outbreak in the spring/summer of 2020, she became interested in writing poetry along with drawing, coloring and wood burning. And yes, the two drawings in the book are her work, along with the photographs. The photo included with the poem Clearing Out The Junk is of one wood burning she did.

Her husband and a friend and fellow author in Sweden, Annika Rolfsdotter, encouraged her and suggested publishing a book and this is the end result!

She hopes you enjoy reading her muses of poetry, prose and fanciful writings as much as she enjoyed writing them.

Made in the USA
Columbia, SC
11 October 2020